Toy Box Subtraction

By Jill Fuller

Consultant
Linda Bullock
Math Curriculum Specialist

Children's Press®
A Division of Scholastic Inc.
New York Toronto London Auckland Sydney
Mexico City New Delhi Hong Kong
Danbury, Connecticut

Designer: Herman Adler Design
Photo Researcher: Caroline Anderson
The photo on the cover shows children subtracting one car from a group
of four.

Library of Congress Cataloging-in-Publication Data

Fuller, Jill, 1949-
  Toy box subtraction / by Jill Fuller.
    p. cm. — (Rookie read-about math)
  Includes bibliographical references and index.
  ISBN 0-516-24423-X (lib. bdg.)   0-516-24673-9 (pbk.)
  1. Subtraction—Juvenile literature. 2. Toys—Juvenile literature.
I. Title. II. Series.
  QA115.F93 2004
  513.2'12—dc22   2004005070

The toy box is too full.

There are too many toys in the toy box. It will not close.

Mike has lots of friends. He invites them to help clean out his toy box. They can have some of his toys.

Mike counts his trucks.
There are 2 trucks.

Mike decides to give the
red truck to Jay. How
many trucks does Mike
have now?

2 trucks – 1 truck

2 trucks – 1 truck = 1 truck

Mike has 1 truck left. It goes back in the toy box.

What can Mike give away now?

There are 4 puzzles in the toy box. Mike gives 2 puzzles to Ellen.

How many puzzles does Mike have now?

4 puzzles – 2 puzzles

4 puzzles – 2 puzzles = 2 puzzles

Mike puts 2 puzzles back in the toy box.

What should Mike give away now?

Mike counts 5 stuffed toys.
The giraffe is the biggest.
He will give the giraffe
to Tim.

How many stuffed toys
does Mike have now?

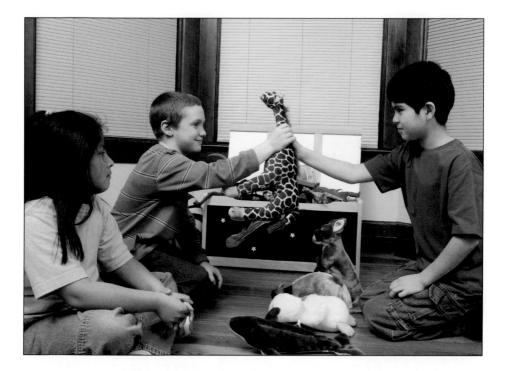

5 stuffed toys – 1 stuffed toy

Mike counts 6 cars in his toy box. He gives the yellow car to Sam. He gives the blue car to Amy.

How many cars are left in the toy box?

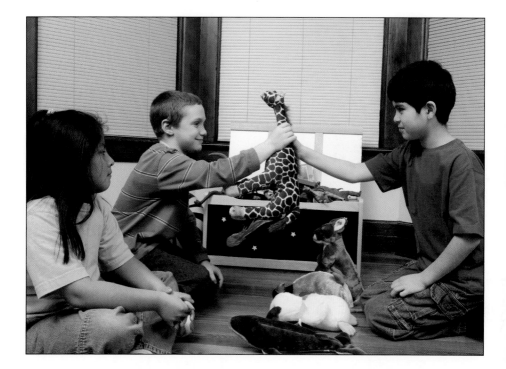

5 stuffed toys – 1 stuffed toy

5 stuffed toys – 1 stuffed toy
= 4 stuffed toys

Mike tries to close the toy box. It is still too full. What will he give away now?

Mike counts 6 cars in his toy box. He gives the yellow car to Sam. He gives the blue car to Amy.

How many cars are left in the toy box?

6 cars – 2 cars

6 cars − 2 cars = 4 cars

The toy box still won't close. Mike counts his plastic dinosaurs next.

Mike counts 7 dinosaurs.
He gives the brontosaurus
and tyrannosaurus to Ann.

How many dinosaurs are
left in the toy box?

7 dinosaurs – 2 dinosaurs

7 dinosaurs – 2 dinosaurs
= 5 dinosaurs

Mike tries to close the toy box. It almost closes. What can he give away now?

Mike thinks hard. Maybe he should give away his beach ball.

No, wait. He will let the air out of the ball!

How many beach balls does Mike have now?

1 beach ball – 0 beach balls

1 beach ball − 0 beach balls
= 1 beach ball

Mike can keep his beach ball! He can also close his toy box. Mike and his friends are happy.

Words You Know

beach ball

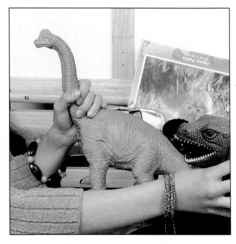

brontosaurus

cars

dinosaurs

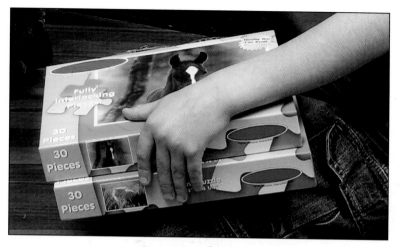

puzzles

toy box

truck

Index

About the Author

Jill Fuller is a teacher, writer, editor, and musician in Taos, New Mexico. She likes math.

Photo Credits